It is our prayer and declaration that you would maintain a Spirit of Integrity concerning the knowledge shared with you in this manual. Meaning, when using the information in this book publicly, you would give author proper recognition and acknowledgement for the knowledge, work, experience, research, and labor of development of this book.

No part of this manual may be reproduced by mimeograph process or by another method of duplication unless expressed written permission has been granted by Charissee Lewis.

Thank You In Advance
for your countenance of righteousness and obedience.

ECCLESIASTES 12:14

For God shall bring every work into judgment, with every secret thing, whether it be good, or whether it be evil.

First Edition: 2018

ISBN: 978-1-934905-98-2

Worldwide Kingdom Publishing
1911 Horger St, Lincoln Park
Michigan 48146
www.drcharisseelewis.com

Building A Strong Prayer Wall

THE POWER OF INTERCESSION

Dr. Charissee Lewis

The violence in America has increased within the last decade. The spirit of lawlessness has reached its peaked throughout many cities in this country, we call the "The Land of the Free." The enemy has positioned his agents in high political positions to pass laws that are contrary to the Word of God. These laws are being passed to cover up and justify satanism, idolatry, perversion, debauchery and immorality. We are definitely living in perilous times, the bible talks about specific events that would occur in the world, to reveal the mark the latter days.

****

II TIMOTHY 3:1-5

This know also, that in the last days perilous times shall come. For men shall be lovers of their own selves, covetous, boasters, proud, blasphemers, disobedient to parents, unthankful, unholy, Without natural affection, truce breakers, false accusers, incontinent, fierce, despisers of those that are good, Traitors, heady, high-minded, lovers of pleasures more than lovers of God; Having a form of godliness, but denying the power thereof: from such turn away.

****

Frankly speaking, as you have read, we are living in the End-Times. Now more than ever, it is time to pray and intercede on behalf of our world, every nation, region, and city. There are so many people who are experiencing devastation, reoccurring problems, and unnatural events. These people need prayer warriors, and intercessors who can pray for them, so God's will can be achieved in their lives and the entire earth realm. God is raising-up new intercessors with a fresh anointing, authority, and ability to carry the weight of the glory; which is required in the ministry of prayer. These intercessors will be bold and courageous to enter the throne room to pray on behalf of those who may need the power of God to intervene in their lives to address various problems. This intercessors will be strong in their faith, the word of God, and they will understand the value of prayer, and will not go to sleep on the prayer wall. They will pray aggressively on behalf of people, cities, countries, nations, situations, and problems so the power of God can intervene to bring rapid solutions.

In reading this book for intercessors, you will be ignited to answer the call of prayer and intercession. The eyes of your understanding shall be enlightened by the revelation that is shared concerning the function and foundation of prayer. We will deal with intricate parts of prayer and what is required to become a true prayer warrior and intercessor. We shall look at the heart of the intercessor and what God expects from him or her in order to be sanctioned to pray. Reader, upon the completion of reading this book, you will receive an impartation from the Holy Spirit to pray in a greater depth of understanding and authority. God is looking for someone who is willing to go deeper in the spiritual realm, to petition him on behalf of someone else. So many people are busy, and to become a true intercessor it takes the agape love of God to open up the heart of the prayer warrior, to cause him or her to pray for people; be it known or unknown. God's love will cause us to move into different dimensions of prayer.

In summary reader, as you open your heart and mind, you will receive new teaching and instructions the Holy Spirit has for you concerning the function, and operation of prayer. You will not be disappointed at the impartation and revelation that shall be transferred to you. Your prayer life shall explode with a reservoir of revelation. This revelation will strengthen you in completing your prayer assignments and building a strong prayer wall for your home, church, and workplace. May God continue to bless you in your secret time of prayer and intercession.

Dedication

This book is dedicated to Intercessors, Prayer Warriors, Watchmen, and Gate Keepers all over the universe; who sacrifice their personal time, and their right to sleep to pray God's will in the earth realm. It is my earnest prayer that you will be refreshed, revived, and ignited to walk in a new mantle of prayer and intercession.

This book is also dedicated to those who are called to the altar, secret place, and/or throne room to pray. My prayer is that you will gain new understanding and prophetic insight into the operation and function of prayer and intercession. There are so many dimensions of prayer in the spirit realm. This book will give you revelation to help you understand what prayer and intercession is all about. I challenge you to heed to the call of prayer and intercession, you will experience great exploits in God, and develop a relationship with God that is so fulfilling it will intimidate the devil and his co-horts. Do not miss your time of intimacy with the Lord, the Kingdom of God needs your intercession.

Special Thanks

A Special thanks, to the Intercession Team of Worldwide Prophetic Kingdom Ministries, I want to say thank you for every prayer you have prayed on behalf of me and my family. Thank you for the unseen, and unheard sacrifices you have made to help build the prayer wall of WPKM.

Thank you to my entire Church family, and the Watch-care Members who carry the burden to pray for WPKM, thank you for remembering us in your prayers. A special thanks to Evangelist Patricia Wilks, one of the Pastors who served as the Prayer Director of WPKM Intercession team from 2010-2018, thank you for building the prayer wall and assisting in the training of new intercessors.

Also special thanks to Elder Durian Williams for your consistency in leading the mid-night prayer, and praying for us.

Special thanks to my Armor bearers/Shepherd's Team who pray personally for me and my family. I thank you for your love, support, and prayers. To Prophet Weshaun Warren who prayed me through the warfare of birthing this book. To Brianna "Sparkle" Warren who was on assignment to assist me the week, God birthed this book through me. Lastly, to Pastor Rudy Jr., thank you for encouraging me to write this book, and praying for me. Thank you for your boldness and your keen prophetic vision, you bring confirmation to major Kingdom Assignments.

Introduction

Do you have a relationship with our Lord & Savior Jesus Christ? Is your relationship with God pleasing to Him? Are you able to hear God in clarity, meaning can you discern when God is talking to you, when the devil is speaking to you, or when your human spirit is speaking to you? It is important as we grow in the Kingdom as believers, that we are able to determine the source of revelation that we are receiving from the spirit realm. There are many voices, and demonic spirits in the Spirit World. These voices are always trying to deceive the perception, hearing, and vision of the believer. Their aim is to deceive the believer into accepting and yielding to the lies of the enemy. So these evil spirits go to great lengths to attack the prayer life of the believer. With that being said, we find it imperative to spend time in prayer.

Prayer is like water to a thirsty man. Prayer is like the blood that runs through the human veins. It is a life force, which needs to be nourished and fed with the proper nutrients in order to produce life. Prayer is that secret place where we commune with the Father. In prayer, we are able to talk to Him intimately, without interruptions or interference. It is that direct line of communication, we are privileged to have as born again believers, specifically, when we speak in our heavenly language, which is a supernatural utterance in an unknown tongue. Prayer is the foundation of creativity. It gives us the power to enter into the throne room of God, and glean from His creative mind to impart ideals to us that have never been seen, or heard of in the universe. Oh how important it is for us to pray! Prayer gives us the spiritual insight and spiritual power we need to function in the Kingdom of God. It destroys the power of darkness, frustrates, and foils the plans of satan and his demonic agents. Prayer gives us the spiritual authority to dismantle every demonic system of satan. It assists believers while increasing our spiritual growth, by accelerating our ability to learn and grasp spiritual content and revelation. It brings healing to the heart of the believer and removes all demonic issues that would hinder our maturation process of spiritual development as breakthrough believers in the Body of Christ.

This society is in dire need of prayer warriors and intercessors that are not afraid to go into the spiritual gates of hell and take back what satan has stolen from God's people. We must teach people how to pray, the purpose of prayer, and how to function and operate in the mantle of intercession. God is developing a new breed of intercessors with keen vision and prophetic insight into the depth of prayer. We find it necessary to share truth concerning the power of an intercessor, in hopes of training and igniting new intercessors with a greater vitality and energy to pray. In spite of all the distractions that have been released from the kingdom of darkness; God has always had a remnant of people who would obey Him and not bow to Baal, the god of this world.

Reader, since you are reading this book there is no question about your spiritual position; you have been called to prayer. The Spirit of God shall woo you in the night season to pray and intercede for people, situations, cities, countries, institutions, and issues that need the deliverance of Our Lord & Savior Jesus Christ. Upon the completion of reading this prayer book, you shall experience a fresh anointing in your prayer life, and you will be able to enter into new dimensions of prayer and intercession. The Lord of Hosts shall endow you with power from the realm of the supernatural to do great exploits in the spirit world. Through reading this prayer book, the Holy Spirit shall teach you secrets in prayer that will increase your ability to persevere and pray through long prayer assignments and issues. He will show you how to develop your spiritual man so you will not experience **"The Burn Out Syndrome of an Intercessor"**. The Burn Out Syndrome of an intercessor occurs when the intercessor becomes weary and tired in the position of prayer. This can happen to any prayer warrior or intercessor who loses focus on their position of prayer. It is easy to be distracted from prayer assignments, when the heart of the prayer warrior and intercessor becomes cold and polluted with pride, anger, and un-forgiveness. It is so important to understand the purpose of prayer so we can build a proper foundation of prayer in our lives as believers. Having a thorough understanding of the mantle of intercession, can assist all intercessors in avoiding and exposing any manifestations of the Burn Out Syndrome. You will not be disappointed as we share knowledge concerning the power of intercession and what is entailed in building a strong prayer wall.

In summary, we recommend that you read this book during your time of personal consecration and prayer before the Lord. It is essential that you read the entire book in order to receive the full impartation of the prayer mantle that the Lord shall release from the pages of this prayer book. We know your prayer life will never be the same, because God is giving you new wineskin, so he can fill your vessel with new wine to pray during this End-Time generation!

****

MATTHEW 9:16-17

No man putteth a piece of new cloth unto an old garment, for that which is put in to fill it up taketh from the garment, and the rent is made worse. Neither do men put new wine into old bottles: else the bottles break, and the wine runneth out, and the bottles perish: but they put new wine into new bottles, and both are preserved.

****

Notes to the readers

It is necessary to share with you the importance of maintaining a consistent prayer life, and activating what you are being taught while reading the contents of this prayer book. Too often, we read but fail to follow through immediately with the prophetic activation, and demonstration of prayer. I pray that you will be inspired and incited to commune with God in every dimension of intercession. We know satan will try to distract, dissuade, and deter you from reading this book, but you must be determined to complete each chapter. There is a supernatural empowerment waiting to be imparted in your prayer life.

Reader do not give up, nor give in, keep your faith and we all shall win! The more intercessors that are activated in the mantle of intercession, the more works we can accomplish for the Kingdom of God. As a result, there shall be an increase of souls saved and snatched from the kingdom of darkness. This new mantle of intercession being revealed and released shall bring healing to the Body of Christ. I truly believe it is an intricate part of God's strategy to dismantle and destroy satan's plans against humanity. There is no doubt we are definitely in spiritual warfare, therefore the prayers of the righteous must increase and avail much.

JAMES 5:16

Confess your faults one to another, and pray one for another, that ye may be healed. The effectual fervent prayer of a righteous man availeth much.

Table of Contents

The ART of PRAYER
(PART ONE)

THE VALUE OF PRAYER: CHAPTER ONE

Do you own something that means so much to you, that it would literally hurt you, if it was destroyed or lost? As human beings, we place so much value on our material possessions; when obsessive, it can be considered a form of idolatry. We spend lots of money, and go through great extremes to protect what we own, because it is valuable to us. The definition of the word "**value**" means to understand the degree of worth, of a thing. It entails the quality of importance, and usefulness of a something that is desirable to you. It is the standard and principles held or accepted. When we study the value of prayer, there is no price that can compare or even match the importance of having a fruitful prayer life. Prayer is so vital to our spiritual walk with God. It is definitely an important method we can communicate with our God. It gives us the life force; we need to survive in the Kingdom of God. Prayer gives us a blueprint on how to live with God in the earth realm. It warns us about the temptations, tricks, and traps of the enemy. Prayer keeps our spirit-man strong and alert to stand against the evil which confronts us on a daily basis. Prayer warriors and intercessors even though we live in this world, the bible has revealed to us we are not of this world. Consequently, the world hates the believers; especially those who are living in holiness, righteousness, and communicating with the Spirit of God on a daily basis. The devil hates the prayer warriors and intercessors who know their purpose and the value of prayer.

****

MATTHEW 26:41

Watch and pray, that ye enter not into temptation:
the spirit indeed *is* willing, but the flesh *is* weak.

JOHN 15:18-19

If the world hate you, ye know that it hated me before it
hated you. If ye were of the world, the world would love
his own: but because ye are not of the world, but I have
chosen you out of the world, therefore the world hateth
you.

****

There is a spirit world that exists and the only way we can gain prophetic insight, and revelation into the spirit world is that we must have a prayer life, and truly comprehend the value of prayer. We have to accept the reality that prayer is our vehicle to communicate with Our Lord & Savior Jesus Christ. Any practice or belief that causes us to draw closer to God, is of the upmost importance, and should be a high priority on our list of life assignments. Unfortunately, there are some Christians who do not know how prayer can enhance their relationship with God, and empower their spiritual walk. Prayer can bring peace in the midst of confusion, and healing where their is heartache. Truly in understanding the value of prayer, it causes us to receive and accept clear spiritual, detailed, workable knowledge that is applicable during our times of prayer and intercession.

Knowing the worth of praying, gives us a greater responsibility to pray and keeps us in divine alignment with God. Prayer warriors and intercessors we must be connected to the Holy Spirit. The Holy Spirit has a personality. He will reveal to us the crucial situations that need our prayers. He is the Comforter, and He brings truth to every situation that is obscure. His illumination shines brightly on the dark areas in our lives and the lives of others. The Holy Spirit brings revelation and prophetic insight to whatever God wants us to know.

****

ROMANS 8:26-27

Likewise the Spirit also helpeth our infirmities: for we know not what we should pray for as we ought: but the Spirit itself maketh intercession for us with groaning which cannot be uttered. And he that searcheth the hearts knoweth what is in the mind of the Spirit, because he maketh intercession for the saints according to *the will of* God.

****

This is why the devil tries every trick of deception; he can use, to impede us from praying. He wants us to accept his lies, by believing that our prayers do not work, in our own lives. We must refute the lies of the enemy, the bible says he is the father of lies and there is no truth in him. Satan is a thief and a robber. He comes to steal, kill and destroy. He wants the people of God to disrespect the laws of God, by disregarding the key elements that prayer brings to the life of a believer. He wants to steal our life of love, joy, peace, happiness, and prosperity in the Body of Christ. He is not our Father, therefore he has no legal right to invade our prayer life, unless we doubt God and believe the lies the enemy suggests and sow into our minds.

****

JOHN 10:10

The thief cometh not, but for to steal, and to kill, and to destroy: I am come that they might have life, and that they might have it more abundantly.

JOHN 8:43-44

Why do ye not understand my speech? even because ye cannot hear my word. Ye are of your father the devil, and the lusts of your father ye will do. He was a murderer from the beginning, and abode not in the truth, because there is no truth in him. When he speaketh a lie, he speaketh of his own: for he is a liar, and the father of it.

****

Prayer warriors and intercessors, you can see in order to know what is occurring in the spiritual realm, we must have a prayer life. Prayer is the vehicle we need to commune with

God. Without understanding the value of prayer, we will not engage in the act of prayer. Therefore, it really is essential for us to esteem prayer as something we cannot live without. My goal is to share truths with you, so you can come to the realization that prayer has to be a part of your very existence! It is valuable! There is no price that could be place on anything that connects us to our God; the quality of prayer is immeasurable to our lives. Realizing the worth of our prayer life causes us to become eager to pray. Therefore, placing the proper value of our prayer life in perspective; it shifts us into *prayer action*. This is the source of our connection with God.

Prayer warrior and intercessor, you will discover quickly when your value of prayer diminishes in your heart and mind; unknowingly, you will open spiritual and natural doors to the sin of **prayerlessness**. Prayerlessness is the sin of not praying. It is walking this spiritual journey without being connected to God. So the less we pray; the less spiritual power we have to operate by faith, and to move in the realm of the spirit. But the more we pray, the greater authority we will gain in the spiritual realm, while receiving the spiritual power and faith to move swiftly in the realm of the spirit. This is why it is essential for ministers to have a prayer life, so we can be sharp and accurate in the realm of the spirit: not slow, inconsistent, and fearful. It is obvious when people are not in alignment in their prayer life, there is dullness in their spirit. This dullness of spirit has a negative affect on the way they function and operate in ministry. This can be very dangerous when working and ministering on the altar. The altar is a place of transformation, where two kingdoms (the Kingdom of God and the kingdom of darkness) fight for the soul of man. Therefore, it is important for us to respect the value of prayer by activating in prayer and intercession consistently.

The sin of prayerlessness also opens the satanic doors to Prayer Killers. Prayer killers are spirits and things we allow in our lives which take away our power to pray. As a result, it causes a direct attack on our relationship with God. Prayer killers isolate us from God, because continual sin brings the spirit of guilt and shame, which hinders us from God. This also brings unwanted demons into our lives. Specifically speaking, it hinders the flow of the anointing, and if you are working the altar it interferes with new souls receiving what they need from God. It also stops the function of the messenger from operating freely in deliverance. The lack of prayer weakens the minister, intercessor, and altar worker which opens spiritual doors for demonic infiltration to invade the atmosphere. This is a major problem of why we do not see the move of God in many of our local churches. As a result, frontline workers, ministers, prayer warriors, and intercessors who really do not value their prayer lives, do not understand how their sin of prayerlessness affects the entire ministry team and the flow of the anointing oil on the altar. People who come to the altar must be able to receive what they need from God, on the altar.

Unfortunately, we have witnessed many people bound as they enter church and bound when they leave church. The problem is many ministers are not in prayer, and they block the flow of the anointing. They hinder the spiritual gifts from operating by releasing a spiritual stench that draws confusion, and negative thinking. The sin of prayerlessness does not just effect you, but it also effects those who are connected to you. Prayer warriors and intercessors, we have a responsibility to communicate with God. Especially, those who are functioning as ministers, and leaders in the Kingdom of God. We must stay prayed up, focused, and continuously maintain a posture of prayer by being diligent in your prayer life! The spirit of distraction is real, and its aim is to destroy your prayer life. It will deceive you into believing everything in your life is more important than prayer. Do not allow distractions, busyness, and laziness to interfere with your value of prayer and your ability to pray!

WE MUST UNDERSTAND THE VALUE OF HAVING A RELATIONSHIP WITH GOD!

WE MUST UNDERSTAND THE VALUE OF PRAYER!

WE MUST UNDERSTAND THE VALUE OF OUR PRAYER LIFE!

Please answer the following questions:

1. How often do you pray?

   _____

   _____

   _____

2. Are you an Intercessor in your local Church?

   _____

   _____

   _____

3. Do you pray on the altar at your Church?

   _____

   _____

   _____

4. How often do you pray on the altar?

   _____

   _____

   _____

5. Do you attend prayer shut-ins?

   _____

   _____

   _____

6. Do you have a specific prayer time?

_____

_____

_____

7. Are you happy with the relationship you have with the Lord?

_____

_____

_____

8. Do you pray for your Spiritual Leaders? (Apostle, Prophet, Evangelist, Pastor, or Teacher) If yes, how often?

_____

_____

_____

9. How often do you pray for your spouse, children, extended family members?

_____

_____

_____

10. Are you dealing with any Prayer Killers, that are interfering with your prayer life? (if yes, write them down)

_____

_____

_____

Understanding The Value of Prayer

Father in the Name of Jesus, I come to You humbly in my spirit. Seeking Your forgiveness from the sin of prayerlessness. I admit I have not really understood the value of prayer. As a result, I allowed prayerlessness and prayer killers to come into my heart and mind, in Jesus' Name. I now realize the value of prayer that I cannot live without communing with You, Father God on a daily basis, in Jesus' Name.

Therefore, I ask You to forgive me and to restore me back in alignment in my prayer life, Jesus' Name. Lord, I repent of my sins and I ask You to sanction me to pray, in Jesus' Name. Grant me the authorization to enter into the secret place where, You share Your secrets with Your servants the prophets, in Jesus' Name. I miss my time with You, and I have been empty, weak, and low spiritually, in Jesus' Name. I rebuke dullness of spirit which is the result of prayerlessness. I rebuke every prayer killer out of my life: disobedience, fear, bitterness, selfishness, idolatry, deception, distractions, doubt, laziness, complacency, unbelief, unforgiveness, devaluing your honor God, stubbornness, and disrespecting myself and other people, in Jesus' Name. I loose purity in my heart and mind, in Jesus' Name. Father God, create in me a clean heart, and renew within me a right spirit, in Jesus' Name. I want to be pleasing unto You, and most importantly I want to be restored in my prayer life. No longer will the enemy isolate me from You, Lord. I submit and surrender my will! I yield to Your Word, because I know You have called me to a lifestyle of prayer. Your word declares to pray without ceasing, according to I Thessalonians 5:17.

Now that I understand the value of prayer, I shall pray willingly and aggressively, without excuses! In the Mighty Name of Jesus Christ, Amen!

THE PURPOSE OF PRAYER: CHAPTER TWO

Do you know your purpose in life? Do you know the reason why God created you? What is your destiny? Everything God creates has a purpose. The word "purpose" reveals the true intentions of a thing, it deals intricately with God's original plan; His reason for creating a person, or thing. When we study the word "prayer", we know prayer is expressing sincere heartfelt words unto the Lord. It is our communication with God.

Prayer is our ability to become one with God which gives us access into the chambers of prayer. When we reach this place in the realm of prayer, we have the power to tap into the divine will and purposes of God to dismantle demonic systems. When a man or woman prays it releases a fire in the spirit world that consumes anything that is not of God. This fire is the Power of God, at work. Prayer is a two way conversation between an individual and God, Himself. So when we observe the purpose of prayer, we have to examine God's intentions for mankind to pray. Why does He wants us to pray?

First of all, God's original plan for man has always been to worship Him. Praying to our Father God in the Name of Jesus Christ is a form of worship; just as serving and giving, is also a form of worship. Man has taken the place of Lucifer in worship; this is why satan hates humanity. From the beginning of creation, everything which entails the creation of man has been supernatural. God created man after the upheaval in heaven. He removed Lucifer and a third of the angels from the Holy

Mountain. Then He created the earth and male and female, and gave them dominion over every kingdom in the earth.

****

GENESIS 1:26-28

And God said, Let us make man in our image, after our likeness: and let them have dominion over the fish of the sea, and over the fowl of the air, and over the cattle, and over all the earth, and over every creeping thing that creepeth upon the earth. So God created man in his own image, in the image of God created he him; male and female created he them. And God blessed them, and God said unto them, Be fruitful, and multiply, and replenish the earth, and subdue it: and have dominion over the fish of sea, and over the fowl of the air, and over every living thing that moveth upon the earth.

****

God formed man from the dust of the ground, and breathed into his nostrils the breath of life; and man became a living soul, Genesis 2:7. God placed the man He formed, in the Garden of Eden and he continued to form and grow trees, and rivers in the Garden. God used Adam to name the animals and then God created a helpmeet for him, and named her Eve. Adam had instructions to follow in the Garden of Eden. But the serpent beguiled them, and Adam was guilty of the sin of disobedience. After the fall of Adam & Eve, Adam lost the

32

relationship God intended for humanity to have with Him, and he and his wife, Eve, was evicted out of the Garden. But thanks be unto God, Our Father; He begotten Jesus Christ who fashion Himself in the likeness of men, and died on the cross so (we), humanity can have a right to eternal life.

****

PHILIPPIANS 2:6

Who, being in the form of God, thought it not robbery to be equal with God: But made himself of no reputation, and took upon him the form of a servant, and was made in the likeness of men: And being found in fashion as a man, he humbled himself, and became obedient unto death, even the death of the cross.

****

In other words, God the Father (the unseen God), took part of Himself, Jesus Christ, (the seen God) and made Him pre-eminent over everything in the universe.

****

PHILIPPIANS 9:10

Wherefore God also hath highly exalted him, and given him a name which is above every name: That at the

name of Jesus every knee should bow, of things in
heaven, and things in earth, and things under the
earth; And that every tongue should confess that Jesus
Christ is Lord, to the glory of God the Father,

****

He died so we can have a right to eternal life. Due to the
fact, Adam's disobedience destroyed the way we communicated
with God; he disrupted the order of communication God
designed for mankind. God created us to co-operate with Him
on earth. Adam's assignment was to bring Heavens Government
to the earth realm. Through Jesus Christ, and receiving the gift
of the Holy Spirit, every man and woman now has the same
opportunity to walk in Governmental Authority, and take
dominion as Adam did. We can decree and declare God's will
over all matters in the earth, and we can do this through prayer
and intercession!

Secondly, the purpose of prayer gives us the ability and
authority to decree and declare Heaven's Government in the
earth realm. As prayer warriors and intercessors, we must
understand our connection with heaven is more than a religious
cliché and mere words that sound appeasing to our ears. There is
a day of judgment where we will stand at the gates of heaven,
waiting to be judged for the life, we have lived here on earth.
There is a present day mandate, an authoritative command that
God assigned us before we left eternity; because He knew us
before we were born in the earth. He purposed our lives to

answer a calling that is far above our comprehension. This calling reveals our true purpose for existence in the earth.

Let us examine Prophet Jeremiah.

****

JEREMIAH 1:4-5

Then the word of the Lord came unto me, saying Before I formed thee in the belly I knew thee: and before thou camest forth out of he womb I sanctified thee, and I ordained thee a prophet unto the nations.

****

Just as God purposed the life of Jeremiah and gave him authority over the Kingdoms. He has given us the same abilities as we commune with Him in prayer.

****

JEREMIAH 1:9-10

Then the Lord put forth his hand, and touched my mouth. And the Lord said unto me, Behold, I have put my words in thy mouth. See, I have this day set thee over the nations and over the kingdoms, to root out, and to destroy, and to throw down, to build, and to plant.

****

Thirdly, the purpose of prayer is to ask God for what we need and want, so we can receive! The bible tells us to seek God's face continually. When we seek Him, we will find Him. Not only does the bible tell us to seek Him continually, but we are suppose to ask Him for whatever we need or want. The purpose of prayer is to ask, so He can answer us. He is sovereign and He wants to answer is children.

****

MATHEW 7:7-8

Ask and it shall be given you; seek, and ye shall find; knock, and it shall be opened unto you: For every one that asketh receiveth; and he that seeketh findeth; and to him that knocketh it shall be opened.

****

The bible assures us if we ask, He will give to us. When we seek His face, we will discover Him. When we knock at the spiritual doors, He will let us in! This means God purposed prayer to give us an avenue to come boldly before Him, in the Name of Jesus Christ and make our requests known unto Him. When a man or woman prays, he or she can receive indescribable blessings; that a prayer-less man or woman will never see in their lifetime. Prayer is going in the presence of God, seeking, asking, and knocking; knowing He will answer our prayers. Genuine prayer and intercession requires the sacrifice and submission of the intercessor. It takes a diligent heart to be consistent in intercession to petition the Lord on behalf of others. As prayer warriors and intercessors, we must understand God answers our requests according to His will, in His process, according to His timing. When we pray we are entering into the timing of God. This is a supernatural realm, where God is in total control. He decides how and when our requests should be answered, according to His plans and purposes for our lives. This is why it is imperative for the prayer warrior and intercessor to understand the power of sacrifice and submission, when functioning in the supernatural realm of prayer. There are times when we intercede and God does not answer the requests as soon as we like; but He answers according to His will. He may require us to pray through an assignment; before He manifests the solution. God is in total control, and the sooner we acknowledge His sovereignty; the faster we position ourselves to be recipients of the prayer requests, we petition before His throne.

ASK GOD!
It is God's will for us to ask Him for what we want, so He can answer our prayers.

A - ASK - We must make a demand in the throne room.......
S - SEEK - We must seek God wholeheartedly...................
K -KNOCK - We must knock until He answers ....

Write the definitions of key words in this chapter.

1. Prayer

    _____

    _____

2. Purpose

    _____

    _____

3. Worship

    _____

    _____

4. Submission

    _____

    _____

5. Mandate

    _____

    _____

6. Commune

    _____

    _____

7. Supernatural

    _____

    _____

8. Comprehension

_____

_____

9. Authority

_____

_____

10. Ask

_____

_____

11. Petition

_____

_____

12. Seek

_____

_____

13. Sacrifice

_____

_____

14. Request

_____

_____

15. Assignment

_____

_____

THE FOUNDATION OF PRAYER:
CHAPTER THREE

Have you ever built anything in your life? Have you ever started anything? Have you ever been in a position of Leadership, where you had to create something new? If you answered yes to any of these questions, then you know that before, you can build or create you must have a **foundation**. A foundation is solid base, where something rests on it; or you can add to it, or build upon it. It is the establishment of something new. A foundation can also be the supporting material, or a part hidden beneath what is being seen by the natural eye. It is a preparation for a structure. When we examine the term *"The Foundation of Prayer"*, we must examine **faith**. Faith is our ability to believe. It is established conviction in unseen things, and hope for a future promise. Faith is a strong belief that God is Sovereign and He is the source of our very existence. Understanding that He is our source, gives us the confidence and the certainty we need to trust God. Faith is the foundation of prayer. It is necessary for us to have so God can solve every problem and answer all of our prayers.

****

HEBREWS 11:1

Now faith is the substance of things hoped for, the evidence of things not seen.

****

Faith and prayer are inseparable, without faith a person cannot pray, and receive an answer from God, because your prayer would be a request that never reaches heaven. We must believe in the God, we serve. He is Alpha and Omega, the Beginning and the End. He is the Author & the Finisher of our faith. Faith is one principle that makes up the foundation of prayer. It is an important quality we need to commune with God. Faith causes us to believe God, before we enter the realm of prayer. It is the key element that causes God to respond to our requests. Faith is established conviction in unseen things and a great anticipation for a future reward. We must believe God, regardless of what we see, feel, hear, or have experienced in our past. With faith in our hearts when we petition His throne, He will answer us. He wants us to believe Him, whole-heartedly. We must be strong in our faith. This is an inner strength and is birth from the spiritual realm, because faith is spiritual. We see the manifestation of faith in the natural when we activate our works. We know faith without works is dead, **James 2:26**.

****

HEBREWS 11:6

But without faith it is impossible to please him: for he that cometh to God must believe that he is, and that he is a rewarder of them that diligently seek him.

****

The scriptures inform us without faith, it is impossible to please Him. When we go into the presence of God, we must believe that He is God, and He can do anything, because He is Sovereign. The latter portion of this scripture tells us God honors diligence, when we seek Him whole-heartedly. This is the spiritual position the bible admonishes us to have when we pray. God honors our consistency in prayer. He wants us to persevere in prayer. As prayer warriors and intercessors, we need the characteristic of diligence, because it reveals our capacity to believe. Diligence in prayer means we are consistent and steady in our efforts to pray. This reveals our level of faith. When people become weak in faith, they stop talking to God and they stop believing. Prayer ignites our believe system, and causes us to trust God in a greater dimension. It becomes an equation of spiritual success. Prayer, faith, and hope equal the promise.

****

MARK 11:22-24

And Jesus answering saith unto them, Have faith in God. For verily I say unto you, That whosoever shall say unto this mountain, Be thou removed, and be thou cast into the sea; and shall not doubt in his heart, but shall believe that those things which he saith shall come to pass; he shall have whatsoever he saith. Therefore I say unto you, What things soever ye desire, when ye pray, believe that ye receive them, and ye shall have them.

PROVERBS 3:5-6

Trust in the LORD with all thine heart; and lean not unto thine own understanding. In all thy ways acknowledge him, and he shall direct thy paths.

****

These scriptures show us, when we release our faith, and trust in God; He will move all obstacles out of our way. Reader have you been taking your problems to God in prayer? Do you believe He can solve your situation? As I stated earlier, faith is the foundation of prayer. It has to be a characteristic in our hearts in order to receive the promises; we petition the Lord for in prayer. Faith is a starting point that opens the door to the spiritual realm, and causes us to connect with God.

In summary, with the problems in America we need faith. The kind of faith that is aggressive, especially when praying through long standing situations. We need our faith to grow and mature. We need faith that is consistent and strong. We know faith cometh by hearing, and hearing by the word of God. However, it is through prayer our faith can be activated and exercised. We must believe God without question. This is the faith that becomes powerful in prayer, because our focus is on Jesus Christ and His ability to move. This makes the problem or petition, a small request for God to answer. It is all in our perception, and ability to see God for who He really is; and faith is the foundation we need in prayer to see a mighty move of God!

Definition of Faith

* Faith is belief that God is Sovereign.
* Faith is unquestioning belief in God.
* Faith is established conviction in unseen things.
* Faith is confidence in God.
* Faith is belief that does not need proof or evidence.
* Faith is trust in God.
* Faith is hope in God.
* Faith is belief in God's Word.
* Faith is certainty that God will do what He promised.
* Faith is resting in God to know He will bring us through all opposition and adversities.
* Faith is thanking God for the bringing us through our past, and trusting that He will take us through our present, and our future.
* Faith is to stand on God's word without compromise.
* Faith is being loyal to God.
* Faith is the opposite of doubt.
* Faith is walking in your spiritual authority.
* Faith is believing your prayers are answered before you pray them.
* Faith is to please God.
* Faith is belief without skepticism and unbelief.
* Faith is believing God is going to do what He promised, without knowing or seeing how He is going to do it.
* Faith is praising God in advance before receiving His promises.

Please answer the following questions:

1. When was the last time you prayed and received your answer within 24 hours?

    _____

    _____

    _____

2. What was the most difficult thing you believe God for and He solved it?

    _____

    _____

    _____

3. How often do you cast your cares upon the Lord?

    _____

    _____

    _____

4. Has anything happened to you to hinder you from believing God? Explain.

    _____

    _____

    _____

5. Write down five scriptures that will ignite your faith?

    _____

    _____

    _____

    _____

6. How do you know when you truly believe God for something you asked Him for?

_____

_____

_____

7. After you pray, do you praise God for your promise?

_____

_____

_____

_____

8. Why is it important to believe God?

_____

_____

_____

_____

9. What is faith to you?

_____

_____

_____

_____

10. Have you ever been in a place where no one could help you and you had to absolutely trust God in the zero hour? Explain

_____

_____

_____

_____

Prayer To Increase Faith

Father in the Name of Jesus Christ, Lord, please forgive me for the sin of unbelief and doubt. I repent before You; I acknowledge I have been weaken in my faith, because I stop praying, and seeking Your face. I ask You, Father God to help me restore my hunger and desire to pray, in Jesus' Name. Lord, increase my faith, in Jesus' Name. I will no longer allow negative thoughts and negative conversations; the opportunity to invade my hearing, in Jesus' Name. I shall cover my ear gates with the word of God. I shall study and listen to Your word, that my faith shall be increased, in Jesus' Name. Father God, thank You for not giving up on me; even when I ignored your call to prayer, in Jesus' Name. I allowed fear, unbelief, laziness, doubt, distrust, rebellion, stubbornness and skepticism to interfere in my relationship with You. I love You Lord, and I bind and rebuke all spirits of fear, doubt, unbelief, laziness, distrust, rebellion, stubbornness, distractions, and skepticism that have hindered my prayer time with You, in Jesus' Name. I loose faith, love, joy, peace, belief, trust, and submission, to You and Your word, in Jesus' Name. Thank You, Lord for a new level of faith and a strong belief system to know You are King of Kings, and Lord of Lords, and everything in the universe belongs to You, in Jesus' Name. Your word declares, "The earth is the Lord's the fullness thereof; the world, and they that dwell therein," according to Psalms 24:1, in Jesus' Name. Therefore, what I bring to You in prayer; I know assuredly, You can fix, solve and resolve all issues, problems, and concerns; You are God! You are the final decision maker! You rule and You reign now and forever, in Jesus' Name. Thank You for a fresh anointing and increased faith,

in the Mighty Name of Jesus Christ!

Amen!

A LIFESTYLE OF PRAYER: CHAPTER FOUR

Have you ever wondered what it means to pray without ceasing? Or what it means to abide in the secret place? In this chapter, we are going to explore the lifestyle of one who loves to pray. A true prayer warrior or intercessor is one who has compassion for souls, and a passion for being in the presence of the Lord. A vessel who has shifted into a lifestyle of prayer is one who is passionate about prayer; this person takes delight in petitioning the throne of grace. To live a lifestyle of prayer, means your intentions and actions revolve around prayer. Prayer becomes the motivation and foundation of your total existence. A prayer warrior or intercessor enjoys talking to the Lord on a daily basis. Being in the presence of the Lord, and petitioning Him is a **prayer action,** this brings the praying vessel great joy. Prayer has to become a necessity in the lifestyle of a prayer warrior. Everyone does not operate in the grace to pray and intercede. There are dimensions in the realm of prayer that are not opened to everyone. We cannot enter into these different spiritual doors, unless the Spirit of God authorizes and allows us to enter in. When people move into spiritual doors and prayer dimensions that God has not sanctioned them to pray in; they are moving into witchcraft and divination. *Witchcraft* means to bend the will of another, to manipulate one, and to coerce one to do what you want without their agreement through demonic powers. *Divination* means to seek information about the future through demonic powers, and explore the supernatural through occult means; be it tarot cards, psychic readings, divining rods, etc.

If God does not give the prayer warrior or intercessor access to enter spiritual portals, then the praying vessel has gained entry, illegally. Illegal entry is a forced entry, a bending which is a form of **manipulation.** This is why, as a prayer warrior and intercessor, it is important that you hear God, in clarity. It is acceptable for you to have a partner in prayer. However, you need to discern the people who want to become your prayer partners; to make sure they have been sanctioned by God to pray in the same realm as you pray. The bible says two are better than one.

****

ECCLESIASTES 4:9-10

Two are better than one; because they have a good reward for their labour. For if they fall, the one will lift up his fellow: but woe to him that is alone when he falleth; for he hath not another to help him up.

MATTHEW 18:19-20

Again I say unto you, That if two of you shall agree on earth as touching any thing that they shall ask, it shall be done for them of my Father which is in heaven. For where two or three are gathered together in my name, there am I in the midst of them.

****

There is power in agreement! As a prayer warrior or intercessor we should be able to identify the grace that you are called to function in, meaning what kind of intercessor are you? What are your areas of prayer? What areas are you anointed to pray in? When the prayer warrior becomes strategic in the ministry of prayer, then there is a greater authority allotted to the vessel of prayer. This is important, because when the prayer warrior does not know his or her prayer dimensions; demons and familiar spirits can attach themselves to the vessel of prayer.

Specifically speaking, people with familiar spirits, hidden agendas, and wrong motives will try to enter the prayer dimension you are in, **illegally**. This is a form of witchcraft, and divination. Prayer warrior and intercessor, I must emphasize the importance of you acknowledging those who connect to you in prayer. As a prayer warrior or intercessor, it is crucial for you to discern the motives of the heart of those whom are connected to you, especially while on major prayer assignments. When there is manifestation of jealousy, negative conversations, negative comments, deception, and pride in other intercessors or people around you: this is an indication that inner healing and deliverance is needed in the heart of the intercessor. Demonic attitudes and negative behavior will hinder a person from entering into different dimensions of prayer. People who display negative attributes need deliverance. We cannot give them access into spiritual doors that are not privy to them. Prayer warriors and intercessors who are stubborn, prideful, and resist inner healing and deliverance can not be trusted in prayer. Do not let these people invade your time of prayer and intercession with the Lord.

A lifestyle of prayer means the praying vessel lives with an attitude of prayer. It means the vessel's heart and mind is positioned in the realm of prayer, and prayer flows out of them like water gushing down a river. The vessel of prayer petitions the throne of God after every activity, without hesitation. There is a boldness that is birth in the heart of this individual of prayer. This person has a set time, where he or she close themselves off from the activities of the world and enter into the prayer chamber. The prayer chamber is a place the praying vessel enters into to reach God, and he or she is cut off from the distractions of the world. It is a place where there is heavy communion with God, and the praying vessel is lifted into a higher dimension of spirituality. It is here the prayer warrior or intercessor has divine hearing, and divine vision. They become opened to the realm of the supernatural. Often times in the prayer chamber, the Holy Spirit will give prophetic insight and revelation into a problem, situation, or concern. He removes confusion, and frustration out of the heart of the intercessor so he or she can pray through a situation and hit the prayer target.

****

PSALM 91:1-2

He that dwelleth in the secret place of the most High shall abide under the shadow of the Almighty. I will say of the Lord, He is my refuge and my fortress: my God; in him will I trust.

****

The prayer chamber is the secret place. It is a place where God whispers His heart to the vessel of prayer. It is a place of purity, a place free from the contamination of witchcraft, divination, perversion, anger, hatred, pride, and jealousy. These are just a few demonic spirits that cannot enter into this realm of the supernatural. When a praying vessel reaches this realm of prayer and intercession, there is a level of purity that continually ignites the passion within the vessel who prays. The more he or she prays the greater the anointing of prayer is released! The prayer warrior and intercessor is endowed with the glory of intercession. This is truly the essence of prayer and the lifestyle of a prayer warrior and intercessor!

In summary, prayer warriors and intercessors be careful, be alert, and be watchful. You have a responsibility to be spiritually aware of your atmosphere. As you are consistent in prayer, your spiritual man will become more sensitive; given you a keenness in your ability to discern people and atmospheres. Your mantle of prayer will increase and ignite your gifts of revelations; the Word of Knowledge, the Word of Wisdom, and the Gift of Discerning of Spirits. These gifts can alert you to the tricks, and traps of the enemy. The bible tells us to watch, as well as pray, according to Matthew 26:41.

MATHEW 26:41

Watch and pray, that ye enter not into temptation: the spirit indeed is willing, but the flesh is weak.

To watch means the prayer warrior has the responsibility of staying awake on prayer duty. This is the assignment of a watchman. A **watchman** is someone who keeps watch, in the realm of prayer. He is a guard in the spiritual realm and he cannot sleep on his prayer post. His post is his ability to carry through his prayer assignment. The watch indicates, there is an enemy lurking to seize a moment of vulnerability.

****

1 PETER 5:8

Be sober, be vigilant; because your adversary the devil, as a roaring lion, walketh about, seeking whom he may devour:

****

PRAYER WARRIORS, INTERCESSORS, AND WATCHMEN DO NOT SLEEP ON THE PRAYER WALL! YOU HAVE A MANDATE TO PRAY THROUGH YOUR PRAYER ASSIGNMENTS AND SOUND THE ALARM WHEN YOU SEE THE DEMONIC ACTIVITY! YOU ARE EQUIPPED TO DESTROY ATTACKS BEFORE THEY MANIFESTS! IT IS TIME TO BUILD A STRONG PRAYER WALL!!!!

If the prayer warrior, intercessor, or watchman sleeps on his posts, he is exposed to the attacks of the enemy. His failure to stay awake and focused while on duty, can endanger those who are under his spiritual jurisdiction. When we study the word "watch", it has many implications and God's revelations.

(1) The heart of the prayer warrior, intercessor, and watchman must be totally and fully awake. This means, the vessel of prayer cannot be a procrastinator, lazy, or slothful. He or she must be spiritually awake; spiritually aware of what's going on in the atmosphere and the realm of prayer. As the prayer warrior and intercessor, abides in the presence of the Lord; he or she will become fiery, anointed, and sharp in operating in the Gifts of Revelation: the gift of discerning of spirits, the word of knowledge, and the word of wisdom.

(2) The mind of the prayer warrior, intercessor, and watchman must be alert, ready, and vigilant. It means the vessel of prayer is required to be quick in their thoughts, and in their actions. They are characterized by vigilance. Being watchful means they are sensitive, observant, and prepared to ward off danger. This is why the purpose of the watchman is crucial to the Body of Christ! When the prayer warrior, intercessor, and watchman is alert he can sound the alarm to the Leaders, so strategy can be activated to destroy the works of satan before he manifests his attacks against the congregation.

(3)   The physical body of the prayer warrior, intercessor, and watchman must be calm, focused, and unassuming. The prayer warrior and intercessor should rest and be refreshed when needed. He or she cannot be desirous of vain glory, by trying to be seen as the best prayer warrior or intercessor in the church. The prayer warrior and intercessor can not be competitive, because competitive behavior opens the door to the works of the flesh; such as emulation and envying. Emulations will occur when prayer warriors and intercessors seek to surpass and out do one another in the realm of prayer. Envying occurs when prayer warriors and intercessors have ill-will towards the blessings of others. This why it is essential for the prayer warrior and intercessor to be secured in God and secured in knowing who he or she is in God. This individual cannot be distracted by the pitfalls of prayer. Also, he or she can not be oppressed by the prayer requests of others. Nor does he entangle himself with the affairs of this life.

In closing, these are **three** important qualities of a praying vessel that has developed a lifestyle of prayer. The spirit, soul, and body of the prayer warrior and intercessor must be in alignment with the will of God, in order to be successful in their time of prayer and intercession.

Prayer For A Lifestyle of Prayer

Father in the Name of Jesus Christ, I come to You with a humble heart, asking You to forgive me for not being a vessel of prayer, yielded to a lifestyle of prayer. I have learned there are specific qualities You expect from me, being an intercessor, as I come before Your throne. Lord, there have been times I have slept on my prayer posts, I allowed my circumstances and situations to distract me from my prayer assignments. I know You have called me to the realm of prayer. There are secrets You want to share with me in the prayer chamber, Father God, I missed the mark in this area; but no longer will I bring a reproach to this position. I ask for Your forgiveness and I seek a fresh anointing. I desire a lifestyle of prayer, let my attitude and mindset be one that prays before I form an opinion. Teach me how to cast my cares in all things. Let the times of refreshing endow me with Your Holy Spirit. Create in me a clean heart and renew in me a right spirit, Father God. Touch my heart in such a way that I will always be awake and alert on my prayer post! Help me to be a calm, focused and unassuming individual in the midst of others. Help me to be strong and to pray through all my prayer assignments; knowing prayer and intercession is a foundational ministry. It is a ministry not made to be seen or heard, but it empowers us to do Kingdom exploits, and causes us to take action. Thank You Father God, as I enter a lifestyle of prayer, I shall walk in a new realm of purity and perseverance in the Mighty Name of Jesus Christ!

Amen

THE MANTLE OF PRAYER: CHAPTER FIVE

Do you know what a mantle is? Furthermore, do you know what is in your mantle? A mantle is a cloak; it is your spiritual covering, which reveals your spiritual position to exercise power, dominion, and authority in the spiritual and natural realm. It reveals who you are in the spiritual realm, so the demons can identify your rank. It also reflects your authorization to exercise dominion in the earth realm. It displays your gifts, weaponry, and your provisions.

The mantle of prayer is the cloak that covers the praying vessel. It is a covering in the spiritual realm, liken unto a blanket which saturates the prayer warrior. It signifies the anointing of prayer which incites the prayer warrior to pray more that the average Christian. It brings an authority to thrust and catapult the vessel of prayer into a prayer dimension that gets results. The mantle of prayer is a grace given by God to the vessel of prayer who has proven he is faithful and consistent in meeting God's requirements of prayer. Prayer leaders are people who are granted this mantle. Prayer to them comes easy and the results are quick, because they abide in a realm of prayer, which is a secret place in the supernatural.

When the mantle of prayer comes into a service or prayer meeting everyone is unctioned to prayer. Prayer in the house of God, is a necessity in this hour. The church of today cannot exists without the mantle of prayer, which causes corporate prayer. The mantle of prayer brings unity in the spirit, it causes a spiritual harmony that a church needs in order to experience the Glory of the Lord in the services. This glory shall open the spiritual portals for the working of miracles. signs and wonders.

The mantle of prayer brings a spiritual covering to the congregation that destroys the assignments of satan. It covers the church from demonic assaults and the spirit of pre-mature death. We are at a crucial time of destruction, there have been demonic attacks launched against churches and the people of God. It will take a mantle of prayer to cover the church of today. We need prayer warriors and intercessors who know how to call down the glory, those who abide in the mantle of prayer. These are men and women of God who understand the value of prayer, they operate in the purpose of prayer and they have built their prayer lives in the foundation of prayer. They live a lifestyle of prayer; therefore they have earned the right to carry the mantle of prayer. We need more prayer warriors who function in this grace.

In closing, I believe God is raising up a new breed of prayer warriors, intercessors, and praying vessels who shall function in this dimension of prayer so profoundly, that it shall birth a revival throughout the land. Praying people, will walk in a strategic level of prayer and intercession where God can trust them with a mantle of prayer; because surely the world is going to need aggressive prayer in the days to come! This level of prayer will usher in the glory of intercession, and we will see more prayer booths, prayer walks, and public display of inter-cessors coming together to pray God's will in the earth realm.

Prayer to Grow Stronger in Prayer and Intercession

Father God, in the Name of Jesus Christ, You are Alpha and Omega, the Beginning and the End. Lord Jesus, I lift You high on today. I esteem You. I extol You, because You are sovereign. You rule and You reign in Your domain. You are King of Kings and Lord of Lords. Father I ask You to take me deeper in Your prayer chambers, that I may learn more of You in the secret place of prayer, in Jesus' Name. I desire to carry the weight of the glory in prayer and intercession, in Jesus' Name. Father God, please show me how to communicate with You, in new dimensions of prayer, in Jesus' Name. Help me to become a prayer leader without the pitfalls of intercession, in Jesus' Name. Holy Spirit, teach me how to become a skilled and anointed intercessor that I may pray God's will in areas people have forgotten about, in Jesus' Name. I want to function in a new authority in my prayer life, in Jesus' Name. I desire to walk in a new measure of love so I can go deep into intimate places in prayer on behalf of others, in Jesus' Name. Lead me and guide me in the spirit, that I may be used to open the gates of heaven and shut the gates of hell, in Jesus' Name. Father God, You can entrust me with Your mantle of prayer, so Your glory can saturate the atmosphere with miracles, signs, and wonders. Father God, Your mantle of prayer provides a covering for Your people. We need Your covering to protect us from satanic assaults. Father God, hide us in You, as we dismantle strongholds, and declare Your will in the earth realm!

In the Mighty Name of Jesus Christ!

Amen

The ART of Intercession
(PART TWO)

THE HEART OF THE INTERCESSOR: CHAPTER SIX

Are you an Intercessor? Do you spend more time in prayer than anything else in your life? Is your heart pure and clean, free from strife and unforgiveness? An intercessor is one who intercedes; one who prays for God's will to be done in the lives of other people. He or she prays for people, problems, crisis, institutions, cities, countries, and regions, this is considered the ministry of intercession. The word **"Intercession"** means *"entugchano"* a Greek term, which means *to chance upon, to confer, to entreat, which is translated as to plead, to appeal.* The aim of the intercessor is to hit the target every time he or she engages in prayer. The intercessor deals with the matters of the Kingdom. He or she is in spiritual connection with Heaven's government. The intercessor has an ear that knows the voice of God and is trained to obey the instructions of God.

****

I TIMOTHY 2:1-3

I EXHORT therefore, that, first of all , supplications, prayers, intercessions, and giving of thanks, be made for all men; For kings, and for all that are in authority; that we may lead a quiet and peaceable life in all godliness and honesty. For this is good and acceptable in the sight of God our Saviour;

****

It is our duty to make supplications, prayers and intercession for those all of mankind, and especially those in authority. When we intercede it brings God's spirit into a situation, allows Him the freedom to do what He wants in the earth realm, because He does not usurp man's will. There are some people who do not know how to pray nor how to reach Jesus Christ. As an intercessor it is our responsibility to pray and intercede on their behalf. Jesus Christ is our example of a great Intercessor. He sits on the right hand making intercession for us.

****

JOHN 14:16

And I will pray the Father, and he shall give you another Comforter, that he may abide with you for ever; even the Spirit of truth: whom the world cannot receive, because it seeth him not, neither knoweth him: but ye know him; for he dwelleth with you, and shall be in you.

****

Wherever there is a need for a divine intervention the intercessor will pray for God's will to superimpose the problem and bring in the solution. An intercessor is an important position in the spiritual realm, because this individual has an assignment to shift situations in the spiritual realm, before they manifest in the natural realm. Therefore the heart of the intercessor must be clean and pure; free from the corruption of sin. The heart of an intercessor has to be filled will the Agape Love of Jesus Christ, an unconditional love, in order to achieve the spiritual assignment of intercession. There is a certain position in which the heart of the intercessor should maintain while serving in a posture of prayer in the Kingdom of God.

The HEART Of An INTERCESSOR

1. **A Heart of Repentance** – This intercessor has a heart willing to acknowledge his or her sins, and quickly turn from sin, once it has been acknowledged. The intercessor with the heart of repentance will not enter the prayer chamber, without repenting first. He or she understands the power of repentance. Repentance can determine the intercessor's ability to hear from God and receive answers to their prayer petitions. The intercessor knows our righteousness is as of filthy rags. Therefore, we must remain humble before our King of Kings.

2. **A Heart of Transparency** – An intercessor with this heart is willing to be honest with God, self and others, about their walk with the Lord. This intercessor will not live a double life, by hiding their true motives. This intercessor is not afraid of opening their heart in the presence of the Lord. This intercessor is opened and transparent about their lifestyle, and they live in alignment with the word of God so their prayers can be heard anywhere, at anyplace, and at anytime.

3. **A Heart of Forgiveness** – The intercessor with this heart is willing to let go quickly all wrongs, oughts and offenses, regardless of the way others has treated them. The intercessor with a heart of forgiveness willingly gives up his or her right to be offended by anyone or any situation. This intercessor's heart is quick to forgive, because he or she understands the power of forgiveness can determine the result of prayers being answered expediently!

4. **A Heart of Humility** – The intercessor with this heart is willing to maintain a position of humbleness, regardless of the number of prayers God answers for them. This intercessor will not allow people to idolize them, because others know he or she can get a prayer through. This intercessor's heart of humility will not allow others to pump him up with pride, to push the intercessor out of position with God.

5. **A Heart of Love** – The intercessor with this heart love others with an unconditional love. This heart is not mean, nor arrogant, nor short tempered. This intercessor does not deal with the spirit of anger. This intercessor is able to intercede for anyone or any situation, because he or she possess the attribute of love. This intercessor do not have respecter of persons nor do they favor certain race, cultures, nationalities, or religions. There is no discrimination or hatred within them.

6. **A Heart of Truth** – The intercessor with this heart has a heart that is open to the spirit of truth. This intercessor's heart is not deceptive. He or she has the ability to discern the real from the fake. This intercessor's heart has vision to see beyond the natural realm, because the heart of truth cannot be deceive by lusts of the eye. This heart has deep perception, and prophetic insight into the depths of the soul of man.

7. **A Heart of Understanding** – This intercessor is *NOT* judgmental, nor critical. The intercessor with this kind of heart can look at all sides of a situation and still pray, regardless of who is right or wrong. This intercessor knows how to intercede without the interference of personal opinions, and the need to be right. The intercessor with this heart is a person of justice, and is truly an advocate called to the throne room of God.

8. **A Focused Heart** – The intercessor with this attribute is focused on completing every prayer assignments, in spite of natural responsibilities. This intercessor's heart is determined to pray through every situation that is before him or her. The focused heart is a person who prays in their own spiritual jurisdiction. They know how to stay in their sphere of authority in prayer. This intercessor will not pray a mist, and will not allow others to pull them into wrong assignments.

9. **A Heart of Discretion** – The intercessor with this attribute can be trusted with the secrets of God. Many personal intercessors must be tried, tested, and proven by God before they are assigned to this realm of intercession. God can trust them with hidden truths about people and situations of utmost important.

10. **A Heart of Servitude** – Every intercessor should be willing to serve, because it takes sacrifice, submission and the ability to serve to be able to pray for others. This intercessor will labor in prayer for hours for others without expecting recognition.

11. **The Heart of the Leader** – Intercessors who function on an Intercessory Team should be connected to the Apostle/ Pastor or Leader of the Church or Organization; so he or she can feel the burden of the Apostle/Leader without communicating with them in the natural. It is crucial to know the "Spirit (Heart) of the Leader you are laboring for in prayer.

12. **A Heart of Purity** – This intercessor's heart is free of darkness, inner hurts, and wounds of the past. This intercessor is free from the spirit of perversion, a spirit that comes to alter what is good, holy, and righteous. The intercessor with the heart of purity will have a fiery prayer with passion and power.

13. **A Heart of Integrity -** This intercessor's heart is filled will strong moral principles. This intercessor is honest and morally upright. This intercessor has a character of consistency and accuracy; he or she will tell you exactly what the Spirit of the Lord is saying concerning you, without adding his or her opinion. A leader can trust an intercessor with a heart of integrity.

14. **A Heart of Discipline -** The intercessor with a heart of discipline will comply to his or her prayer time with the Lord. He or she has zero tolerance for distractions that may try to interfere with his or time of prayer. This intercessor usually has a schedule time for prayer and stick to it on a daily basis. This intercessor automatically wakes up even if their prayer time is during the third watch (12:00a.m.- 3:00a.m.) or the fourth watch (3:00a.m. - 6:00a.m.). This intercessor operates with temperance, one of the fruits of spirit.

15. **A Balanced Heart -** The intercessor with a balanced heart is one who knows all to juggle the responsibilities of life with their responsibilities as an intercessor. This intercessor does not engage in flaky intercession; nor does he or she exalt themselves over their Apostolic Leader. They understand the scriptures in **Proverbs 11:1-2** *"A false balance is abomination to the Lord: but a just weight is his delight. When pride cometh, then cometh shame: but with the lowly is wisdom."*

Intercessors the previous descriptions, are the attributes we should possess in our hearts as active intercessors on the front line of ministry, in the Kingdom of God. It is imperative for our hearts to be in alignment with the word of God, so our character can become a reflection of the image of Jesus Christ. The heart of the intercessor must be whole, and healthy in order to be effective in the posture of prayer for others. Intercessors know this, before anything happens or manifests in the natural realm, it was birth in the realm of the spirit first. Therefore it is essential for intercessors to be healed in our hearts, so we can receive clear revelation in prayer from the Holy Spirit: be it visual or communicative. God expects the intercessors to pray and intercede for issues we see, hear, and know need the divine intervention of God. We must purge ourselves from worldly and fleshly behaviors, that will try to corrupt our hearts and infiltrate our minds to stop us from praying through our prayer assignments. As intercessors, we have a crucial job to intercept demonic onslaughts that may try to impede God's will in the earth. This is why our hearts must be made whole, so we can discern the revelation with a true heart that is pleasing unto the Lord!

INTERCESSORS ....

Keep thy heart with all diligence: for out of it are the issues of life.

Proverbs 4:23

WRITE DOWN THE KIND OF HEART YOU HAVE AS AN INTERCESSOR AND EXPLAIN YOUR CHOICE:

_____

_____

_____

_____

_____

_____

_____

_____

_____

_____

THE HEART OF THE INTERCESSORS THAT NEEDS HEALING/DELIVERANCE:

* An Angry Heart
* An Anxious Heart
* A Backbiting Heart
* A Black Heart
* A Bitter Heart
* A Broken Heart
* A Cold Heart
* A Corrupt Heart
* A Critical Heart
* A Deceptive/Lying Heart
* A Demonic Heart
* A Disobedient Heart
* A Disrespectful Heart
* An Evil Heart
* A Fearful Heart
* A Insecure Heart
* A Jealous Heart
* A Judgmental Heart
* A Lustful Heart
* A Rejected Heart
* A Revengeful Heart
* A Perverted Heart
* A Prideful Heart
* An Unforgiving Heart
* A Wicked Heart
* A Wounded Heart

INTERCESSOR'S ASSIGNMENT

On the previous page, we shared some attributes of the heart of an intercessor which indicates a need for inner healing and deliverance. Please identify and write down any of these attributes that are operating in your life, so you can go through proper inner healing and deliverance, before engaging in any kind of prayer assignments and spiritual warfare.

_____

_____

_____

_____

_____

_____

_____

_____

_____

The CHARACTER Of An INTERCESSOR

Here are a few characteristics of an Intercessor.

- ✓ Humble
- ✓ Bold in the Spiritual Realm
- ✓ Faithful
- ✓ Focused
- ✓ Integral
- ✓ Importune
- ✓ A team player
- ✓ Servant
- ✓ Giving
- ✓ Loving
- ✓ An Environmental Change Agent
- ✓ Prophetic
- ✓ Able to see in the Spirit
- ✓ Passionate about prayer
- ✓ Love to see the will of God accomplished in the earth
- ✓ Discrete
- ✓ Proactive
- ✓ Unselfish
- ✓ Honest
- ✓ Love to see people free from demonic oppression
- ✓ Forgiving
- ✓ Diligent
- ✓ Complete prayer assignments
- ✓ Knows the word of God
- ✓ Spiritual minded
- ✓ Fair/Spirit of Justice

INTERCESSOR'S ASSIGNMENT

Write down the characteristics that you have:

_____

_____

_____

_____

_____

_____

Write down the characteristics you need to develop or work on:

_____

_____

_____

_____

_____

_____

Write down your how your heart affects your ability to hear revelation from God:

_____

_____

_____

_____

_____

_____

DIFFERENT KINDS OF INTERCESSORS: CHAPTER SEVEN

There are different kinds of Intercessors, because there different dimensions in prayer. God is awesome in how He structured the realm of prayer and the ministry of intercession. We are without excuse, when it comes to communicating with Him. He does not expect us to function in the same realm the same way. He made us all different. He has given us a *"special blend"*, meaning everything that makes us who we are, can be used in the realm of prayer and intercession. The way we look, how we talk, our countenance and disposition; God uses in the realm of prayer and intercession. As intercessors, we have to discover our grace and where He has fashioned us to function in the Kingdom of prayer. Do you know what kind of intercessor you are?

First of all, there are different kinds of prayers, and sometimes certain prayers call for a specialist to pray and intercede. It depends on the petition: be it a person, place, situation or problem. Some intercessors become a spiritual authority in a specific area of prayer, because they have battled and triumph over the enemy in that particular area. So it may be an area, they are call to intercede in; meaning, once you gain victory in a difficult place in your life, you can become a candidate to intercede on behalf of others.

One of the greatest experiences in intercession is praying

for someone or a situation and witnessing their victory over the adversary. As an intercessor, when the Lord captures and transforms your heart; it hurts you to see anyone oppressed and bound by pain and demonic spirits. As a result, a true intercessor will become committed to his or her prayer assignment to ensure the freedom of one bound by satan. The ministry of intercession requires sacrifice, submission, and servitude from the intercessor. This is not an area of ministry for the weak or faint in heart. The intercessor must be diligent, and dedicated to the call of prayer with a heart of faith. **Faith** is a requirement for the intercessor to enter any dimension of intercession and complete the assignment of prayer. It is an amazing encounter for the intercessor to engage in intercession, and then witness the result of their intercession, as successful. The more the intercessor prays the more he or she will desire to pray, and the anointing of intercession increases on the intercessor's life in that specific area of prayer. When the intercessor continually intercedes successfully, he or she gains spiritual knowledge, increased faith, and strategies to conquer the enemy in that area of prayer.

LUKE 12:48

But he that knew not, and did commit things worthy of stripes, shall be beaten with few stripes. For unto whomsoever much is given, of him shall be much required: and to whom men have committed much, of him they will ask the more.

In Cindy Jacobs, <u>Possessing the Gates of the Enemy</u> she lists **five** types of Intercessors:[1]

1. General
2. Crisis
3. Warfare
4. Personal
5. Specialist

During prayer the Spirit of the Lord revealed more types of intercessors. We listed them as well, and shared their function in depth.

6. Apostolic Prophetic Intercessor
7. Church Intercessor
8. Commando Intercessor
9. Kingdom Intercessor
10. Private Intercessor
11. Prophetic Warfare Intercessor

---

[1] Cindy Jacobs, Possessing the Gates of the Enemy

DIFFERENT KINDS OF INTERCESSORS

❖ **Intercessor** – An intercessor is one who prays and intercedes on behalf of someone else, be it situations, cities, countries, regions, or nations. An intercessor will pray so God's will can intervene in any problem or situation. The intercessor aim is to pray His will to be done in the earth realm. **I Timothy 2:1-2**, *I exhort therefore, that, first of all, supplications, prayers, intercessions, and giving of thanks, be made for all men; for kings, and for all that are in authority; that we may lead a quiet and peaceable life in all goodliness and honesty.*

❖ **Apostolic Prophetic Intercessor** – This intercessor is one who prays concerning the matters of the Kingdom. Their thrust of prayer is to bring in the Apostolic Prophetic anointing into a specific region or church; so Kingdom Advancement may be accomplished in the earth realm.

❖ **Church Intercessor** - This intercessor is prayer assignment is to pray specifically for the church, and the vision of the Church. Usually, you will find this intercessor shutting in the church, and praying on the altar. The Church Intercessor has a burden to birth the vision of the church and to create a healthy spiritual climate that is conducive for miracles, signs, and wonders.

The bible talks about Anna the Prophetess who prayed in the temple, the book of **Luke 2:36-37,** *And there was one Anna, a prophetess, the daughter of Phanuel, of the tribe of Aser: she was of great age, and had lived with an husband seven years from her virginity; and she was a widow of about fourscore and four years, which departed not from the temple, but served in fastings and prayers night and day.*

❖ **Commando Intercessor** – A commando is an intercessor who has the anointing, authority, skill, and sanction to move into all dimensions of prayer. This intercessor is seasoned and lives a lifestyle of consecration and adoration before the Lord; so he or she can be used anyplace, anywhere, at anytime to intercede for his or her prayer assignment. This intercessor lives a lifestyle ready and equipped to enter any dimension of prayer.

❖ **Crisis/Emergency Intercessor** – This intercessor prays in times of drama, traumatic situations, and life or death situations. This intercessor symbolizes a person who works in the emergency room in a hospital. He or she feels the burden of disastrous situations, chaos, and mayhem; and he or she prays until the burden of intercession is lifted. Their mantle of intercession rises in times of trouble. This intercessor can hear bad news on television, the social media, or through conversation and he or she will begin to pray and intercede for God's divine intervention.

❖ **Gap Dweller** – A gap dweller is one who will bridge the gap, where there has been a breach in covenant, the gap dweller will pray until the hedge is restored. **Ezekiel 22:30,** *And I sought for a man among them, that should make up the hedge, and stand in the gap before me for the land, that I should not destroy it: but I found none.*

❖ **Gate Keeper** – A gate keeper is one who controls the spiritual gates of the congregation. The gate keeper regulates the spiritual flow of the traffic in the church. He or she is security, in the spiritual realm and he allows the right people to enter the gates of the church. Therefore, the gate keeper gift of discerning of spirits must be keen.

❖ **General Intercessor** – This intercessor can pray in general areas of intercession. They have no specialty or particular area of prayer. They can pray with or without an assigned prayer list. This level of intercessor is a basic level of intercession.

❖ **Kingdom Intercessor** - This intercessor prays specifically for matters of the Kingdom of God. This intercessor has an anointing to birth Kingdom Churches and Ministries. This intercessor is gifted in praying for a shift from the pastoral anointing into the Apostolic anointing so churches can function in Kingdom of God with kingdom principles.

❖ **Personal Intercessor** – The personal intercessor is an intercessor assigned to pray for a man or woman in the Five-Fold Ministry. This intercessor has a heart of discretion where the Spirit of God can trust them with the secrets of the person he or she is assigned to pray for; this is a position of honor and high esteem in the spiritual realm.

❖ **Prayer Warrior** – A prayer warrior is one who specializes in warring in the realm of the spirit in prayer. This person is skilled and anointed in spiritual warfare, and he or she knows how to go to battle in the spiritual realm. The prayer warrior usually operates with the gift of discerning of spirits. He or she must be able to identify the nature of demonic spirits to demolish demonic systems and destroy demonic assignments.

❖ **Private Intercessor** - This intercessor prays concerning private matters. He or she is entrusted with top secret information and revelation from God and man. The private matters can be confidential issues in the workplace, church, or home. The prayer assignments of a private intercessor can also includes matters of the heart, issues in the marriage, or family secrets. The private intercessor can be trusted to pray without uttering a word to anyone else.

❖ **Prophetic Warfare Intercessor** – The prophetic warrior is one who wars in the prophetic realm and decrees and declares God's prophetic mind over a situation, circumstance or person. This intercessor has a prophetic anointing which gives him prophetic insight to see the future plans of God and war it through in prayer.

❖ **Specialist Intercessor-** The specialist intercessor is a person who specializes in a particular area subject of prayer. This intercessor is considered an expert in the subject he or she is called to pray in. This intercessor has the anointing, authority, ability, and authorization to pray in this specific area.

❖ **Spiritual Warfare Intercessor** – This intercessor is not afraid of demonic spirits. He or she specializes in the ministry of deliverance. This intercessor has a keen gift of discerning of spirits. He or she understands the character and nature of the demonic spirits which is imperative when warring in the realm of darkness. This intercessor must be brave and anointed to identify, confront, and annihilate demonic systems. They are not afraid to engage in battle in the spiritual realm and destroy demonic plots. They specialize in tearing down the kingdom of darkness, pulling down strongholds, destroying generational curses, and dismantling demonic systems.

❖ **Watchman** – The watchmen who prays is usually a prophet or minister who keeps watch. He guards the fold spiritually, by praying on post at a specific time and place. His duty is to detour and destroy anything that would endanger the congregation. He is a seer in the spirit and he can see into the future.

Men and women of God study the different kinds of intercessors and pray and ask God, what realm of intercession He has called you to; and begin to intercede in that dimension of prayer. God purposed for you to read this book to impart to you revelation and impartations to enhance your prayer life and the your ministry of intercession. There is no room for doubt or apprehensiveness, you must answer the call of intercession there is an urgency for you to get in alignment concerning the realm of prayer and intercession. The Holy Spirit wants God's people to become skilled and anointed in specific realms of intercession. We must master the art of prayer and intercession. This is important for you to know, when you are assigned to build a strong prayer wall!

A MESSAGE FROM THE HOLY SPIRIT

"INTERCESSOR, I AM CALLING YOU TO COMMUNE WITH ME. I WANT YOU TO BUILD OUR INTIMACY THROUGH RELATIONSHIP AND THE FELLOWSHIP. I AM WAITING FOR YOU TO ENTER INTO THE PRAYER CHAMBER TO BASK WITH ME. THERE IS MUCH TO SHARE WITH YOU CONCERNING YOU AND THOSE AROUND YOU. I AM WAITING TO MEET YOU IN THE SECRET PLACE DO NOT TARRY FOR TIME IS OF THE ESSENCE AND HEAVEN WANTS TO HEAR FROM YOU, NOW!!!!!!!"

YOU ARE CALLED TO PRAYER AND INTERCESSION!!!!! MEET ME IN THE SECRET PLACE, SAITH THE LORD OF HOSTS!!!!!

THE LANGUAGE OF THE INTERCESSORS: CHAPTER EIGHT

Every profession has its own vernacular to convey and to relate to; a language to communicate with others who operate in the same field of profession. For instance, a doctor has medical terminology, a lawyer has legal terminology, and a musician has musical terminology. In studying the ministry of intercession, the intercessor also has a language which ignites change in the realm of the spirit. When the intercessor uses the language designed specifically for the function of intercession, it accelerates God's process of divine intervention to bring a solution to any problem or situation of concern. It is very important for the intercessor to understand his or her function, and operation in the ministry of intercession. Understanding the language of intercession, allows the intercessor the ability to maximize his or her full potential while praying and interceding. In this chapter, we will examine some terms of intercession used to bring understanding and enlightenment to those who have been called to the ministry of intercession. These terms will guide the intercessor into a greater depth of prayer, causing the intercessor to become skilled in the realm of prayer. On the next few pages, we will share some common terminology that intercessors may use while functioning in prayer and intercession. We will share scriptures and definitions, to enlighten the intercessor on the purpose of the terms and phrases when discussing and operating in the realm of intercession.

❖ Binding and Loosing

- **Matthew 16:19**

    And I will give unto thee the keys of the kingdom of heaven: and whatsoever thou shalt **bind on earth** shall be **bound** in heaven: and whatsoever thou shalt **loose on earth** shall be **loosed in heaven**.

- God has given us keys to the kingdom to bind and to loose, we have the ability to shut the gates of hell and open the heavens to allow God's will to come into the earth realm.

- These keys can represent authority given by God to use to assist us in opportunities to bring people into the Kingdom of God. We can use these keys to intercede and release others who are bound by demonic powers.

- When the intercessor binds the enemy, we stop his onslaughts from attacking us.

- When we loose we are releasing God's will to enter the situation we are praying for.

- The scripture reveals a backing from heaven, because whatever is done on earth, it has been established in heaven first.

- What God has done in the spiritual realm cannot be reversed, changed, or altered unless God changes it!

❖ **Destroying the Yoke or Breaking the Yoke**

- **Isaiah 10:27**

  And it shall come to pass in that day, that his burden shall be taken away from off thy shoulder, and his yoke from off thy neck, and **the yoke shall be destroyed because of the anointing.**

- A **yoke** is something that binds, unites or connects; it put things together.

- It is a **coupling instrument** that symbolizes forced labor. It brings oppression and causes people do things against their will.

- In order for intercessors to have the ability to destroy yokes, we have to consecrate ourselves before the Lord and believe God. *Matthew 17:20-21, And Jesus said, Because of your unbelief: for verily I say unto you, If ye have faith as a grain of mustard see, ye shall say unto this mountain, Remove hence to yonder place; and it shall remove; and nothing shall be impossible unto you. Howbeit this kind goeth not out but by prayer and fasting.* Fasting and praying will always destroy a yoke.

- Fiery prayers and aggressive prayers that are effectual and fervent will achieve the result of destroying the yoke.

❖ **<u>Pulling Down Strongholds</u>**

- **II Corinthians 10:4-5**

  (For the weapons of our warfare are not carnal, but mighty through God to the pulling down of **strongholds**;) Casting down imaginations, every high thing that exalteth itself against the knowledge of God, and bringing into captivity every thought to the obedience of Christ;

- We can use God's mighty weapons to defeat the enemy when we are in spiritual warfare. The intercessors can use the weapon of the Word of God and the expertise of the Holy Spirit to give them strategies in prayer to **pull down the strongholds.**

- A **stronghold** is a fortified place that satan builds to deceive and exalt himself against the knowledge of God.

- A **stronghold** is also a fenced area in our minds, that causes us to react and respond in a behavior that is contrary to the word of God.

- As intercessors, in order for us to pull down the strongholds; we must identify the **strongman**, who sits at the gate of the mind to keep the stronghold in place. Once we cast out the strongman, we can spoil his goods.

❖ **Praying Through**

- **I Thessalonians 5:17**
  Pray without ceasing.

- Pray without ceasing means to have a spirit of prayer. This requires the intercessor to train his or her spirit to pray, even when the physical body does not want to pray.

- An intercessor can train his or her spirit to pray even while they are sleep.

- **Pray without ceasing** means to have a heart that is thankful. It means to have an attitude of prayer.

- As intercessors, we must be **persistent in prayer** until we have the assurance from God that His will has been accomplished concerning the prayer assignment.

- In order to pray through, the intercessor must be **persistent in prayer**. Meaning he or she must refuse to give up, even though one may be faced with danger, opposition, or difficulty.

- The intercessor must become aggressive in the continuance of prayer concerning that prayer assignment. There is an innate ability that will not allow the intercessor to stop until they have the sanction from God to stop.

KEY WORDS FOR INTERCESSION

Abolish	Destroy
Annihilate	Demolish
Assist	Dismantle
Advance	Fight
Break	Flee devil
Break into new realms	Foil
Break out	Frustrate the plans of the enemy
Breakthrough	Impede over
Break down	Prevail
Beat down	Prevent
Cast out	Root out
Cast down	Smash
Chase	Smite
Confound	Stop
Confuse the enemy	We curse the works of satan
Contend	We cancel the assignment of satan
Consume	We thwart off the enemy

THE POWER OF THE INTERCESSION: CHAPTER NINE

The power of intercession has the ability to change the world. It can change a city, country, nation and government. When people pray, it changes the heart of those whom we are praying for. There is a clarion call to pray and intercede for our leaders, and those who are in authority that we may lead a quiet and peaceable life. God is raising up a new breed of intercessors who will change the course of this universe, because they are in alignment with heaven's government. They are in tuned with the move of the Holy Spirit, and they shall be used to birth the spirit of revival throughout this land. These intercessors are bold; they are not afraid to pray privately and publicly. They are aggressive in the function of prayer and intercession. Their prayers are effectual and fervent, able to reach heaven to receive an answer from God quickly. These intercessors understand the purpose and value of prayer. They are skilled and anointed in the operations of intercession. They understand the importance of talking to God. They pray on a consistent basis. They value their time of intimacy with the Lord. These intercessors will walk in the weightier dimensions of prayer, intercession, and the gifts of the spirit. This will give the intercessor supernatural authority to shut down demonic systems in the spiritual and natural realm. Frankly speaking, these intercessors will be endowed with the power of intercession. The power of intercession has a supernatural authority to drive forth the power of God in the earth realm!

As intercessors, when we pray in the power of intercession, it allows us to enter into new spiritual portals and new realms of the supernatural: where we can be suspended in time. Intercessors it is not uncommon to be translocated, caught up in the spirit, through trances. God allows the intercessor to see a glimpse of what His will and solution is, for the situations and people we may need intercession. Through the power of intercession, we will are given access into these various dimensions in the spirit realm. God has always had a remnant of people who will serve Him, regardless of what is taking place in the world. The anointing in the ministry of intercession shall intensify upon those who will abide in the secret place. The intercessors who maintain a posture of prayer in the secret place of the most High will always be covered in the midst of persecution, opposition, and seasons of warfare. There is a fresh glory being endowed from the heavenlies into the spirit of the intercessors who are willing to sacrifice even more time in their prayer chambers.

****

PSALM 91:1-2

He that dwelleth in the secret place of the most High shall abide under the shadow of the Almighty. I will say of the LORD, He is my refuge and my fortress: my God; in him will I trust.

****

This is an hour were supernatural prayer mantles are being released throughout the land. With this fresh oil of prayer, we are going to witness the move of God on the college campuses, in the marketplace, and on the streets. The glory of God is sending people out of the churches and into the cities and regions, where folks really need a divine intervention; but they are too bound and oppressed by satan to move. The power of intercession is going to dismantle and dethrone the enemy's plots and plans in this end-time move of the Holy Spirit. We are getting ready to witness some undocumented miracles. This End-time move will be ignited and blazed up through effectual fervent prayer.

****

JAMES 5:16

Confess your faults one to another, and pray one for another, that ye may be healed. The effectual fervent prayer of a righteous man availeth much.

****

In summary intercessors, I want to encourage you to continue to move in the power of intercession, because as you pray it will change the course of this nation. Truly, in the days to come we will hear throughout the land, how the power of intercession has cancelled pre-mature deaths and allow the Glory of God to consume the atmosphere. Miracles, signs and wonders shall be released supernaturally through the power of intercession.

94

INTERCESSOR'S PRAYER POINTS:

- ❖ Pray for your Family/other Families
- ❖ Pray for your Marriage/other Marriages
- ❖ Pray for your Children/all Children
- ❖ Pray for the Kingdom of God/Kingdom Advancement
- ❖ Pray for your Church/Ministry
- ❖ Pray for Souls To Be Saved
- ❖ Pray for the Apostles, Prophets, Evangelists, Pastors, and Teachers
- ❖ Pray for Men/Women
- ❖ Pray for Single Parents
- ❖ Pray for your Neighborhood/other Neighborhoods
- ❖ Pray for your City/other Cities
- ❖ Pray for the President/Government
- ❖ Pray for the House of Representatives/House of Senate
- ❖ Pray for the Courts/Judges/Jurors
- ❖ Pray for the Police departments
- ❖ Pray for the Water
- ❖ Pray for America/all Continents
- ❖ Pray for the Educational system/Principals/Professors/ Teachers/Students
- ❖ Pray for the Healing from Sicknesses/Diseases/Infirmities
- ❖ Pray for the Hospitals/Doctors/Patients
- ❖ Pray for the Kingdom of God
- ❖ Pray for your Destiny/Purpose/Mandate
- ❖ Pray for Prosperity
- ❖ Pray for Spiritual Growth
- ❖ Pray for Deliverance from Demonic Spirits
- ❖ Pray for the Truth
- ❖ Pray for Inner Healing
- ❖ Pray for Intercessors in every country

BUILDING A STRONG PRAYER WALL:
CHAPTER TEN

The Church that is going to operate in a new Glory that is being released from Heaven, is a praying church. The church of today, cannot survive the assaults of satan in this hour without a strong intercession team. The wineskin of formalism and ritualistic religious prayer meeting are out of tune with the will of God. Shallow prayers will not survive the plots of the devil. We need strong prayer warriors and intercessors that are not afraid to enter the realm of intercession to persevere in prayer. Prayer warriors and intercessors who are diligent in prayer. Today's church needs the fire of the Holy Spirit to assist in building a strong prayer wall against the attacks of the enemy. In order for the prayer wall to be solid, the intercessors must become strong by connecting with the vision of the Church. This connection which is a form of submission is imperative, so the intercessor can understand the mandate God has given their Apostle/Leader. It is essential for the prayer warrior and intercessor to honor God and their Spiritual Leadership, in order for their prayers to be answered. Submission and obedience to God and your Spiritual Leader speaks volumes about one's character and authority in the spiritual realm. When the prayer warrior and intercessor are disobedient to God and their Apostle/Spiritual Leader, it opens them up to the realm of witchcraft. This means their prayers are unauthorized, contaminated, empty, and impure. It does not matter how well a prayer warrior or intercessor may sound in prayer, God is looking at the motives of the heart. In chapter six, we discussed the heart of the prayer warrior and intercessor. It is crucial for all prayer warriors and intercessors to be humble, obedient and have the right heart disposition; in order to remain in alignment while functioning in the ministry of intercession.

****

I SAMUEL 15:22-23

And Samuel said, Hath the LORD as great delight in burnt offerings and sacrifices, as in obeying the voice of the LORD? Behold, to obey is better than sacrifice, and to hearken than the fat of rams. For rebellion is as the sin of witchcraft, and stubbornness is as iniquity and idolatry. Because thou hast rejected and the word o the LORD, he hath also rejected thee from being king.

****

When the prayer warrior and intercessor commune with God, and understands the vision of the church, the Holy Spirit then increases his or her capacity to pray, by giving them the grace to engage in intercession. With this grace comes the power to intercede, the prayer warrior and intercessor is endued with the power of intercession; which is the authority, anointing, and ability to build a strong prayer wall.

The purpose of the prayer wall is to protect the Church, the Leader, the congregation, and all the work that is under the leadership of that Apostle, Prophet, or Pastor. When an intercessor becomes an effective builder of the prayer wall, it is because he or she understands his assignment as an intercessor. The intercessor must know his tasks of prayer, and remain committed to the fulfill his prayer assignments. This means he needs to have a clear understanding concerning his spiritual jurisdiction of prayer. Every intercessor is given a sphere of authority in the spiritual realm. Knowing exactly what God wants him to pray for, and staying persistent to that prayer assignment, will give him rank in the spirit realm to increase his authority as an intercessor on the wall. His ability to persevere and pray through his prayer assignments, and stay in alignment in the spiritual realm, will advance him into a higher dimension and spiritual authority in prayer.

Secondly, the intercessor must live a lifestyle in alignment with the characteristics of an intercessor, which we also discussed in chapter six. The characteristics are guidelines that gives us a list so we can examine what is in the heart of an intercessor. The intercessor has to operate in the fruits of the spirit; especially the fruit of temperance, to be able to fast and pray at times when others are celebrating worldly holidays. This means the intercessor is required to consecrate when God calls for a consecration without questions and apprehension. The lifestyle of the intercessor is essential to the advancement of the intercession in the realm of the spirit. When the intercessor can enter in the throne room of God free from sin, it positions the intercessor to receive results in prayer expediently. The bible tells us in Hebrews 4:16, *"Let us therefore come boldly unto the throne of grace, that we may obtain mercy, and find grace to help in time of need."*

Lastly, the intercessor is required to have structure. This structure deals with the intercessor's ability to stay on the prayer wall, regardless of opposition and adversity. He has to live a lifestyle of agreement with the Holy Spirit. The intercessor's belief system must constantly be in alignment with the Spirit of God, to ensure spiritual and natural protection of the intercessor. This means the intercessor's obedience is essential in maintaining divine protection from the enemy in spiritual and natural realm. When the intercessor follows the protocol of intercession; he or she will be given an increase of anointing to rule on the prayer wall. With this anointing the intercessor is assigned new angelic support to keep him always covered on the prayer wall. Therefore, with the covering of God and the covering of the Spiritual Authority assigned to his life; be it Apostle, Pastor or Spiritual Parents, etc; the intercessor will always be protected.

In summary, I encourage you, intercessors to stay on the prayer wall. Continue to pray regardless of what the enemy may be saying or doing. You have been called to pray and to intercede do not allow satan to distract you and discourage you from your source of power. Your ability to pray and intercede is the vehicle God will use to advance you in the Kingdom! I declare and decree your ability to pray and intercede shall increase in the days to come and you shall be used to build strong prayer walls for the church you attend, and the Glory of God shall follow you wherever you go! You must invade the gates of hell through the power of intercession and building a strong prayer wall to protect the work of the Kingdom of God!

INTERCESSORS.....
BUILD A STRONG PRAYER
WALL THROUGH THE
POWER OF
INTERCESSION!!!!!

Prayer For Salvation

Father in the Name of Jesus Christ, Lord I ask You to forgive me for all my sins, sins knowing and unknowing. Today, I denounce satan out of my life. I repent of any association with the spirit of lucifer, witchcraft, and jezebellic spirits. Lord, I want to be saved, sanctified, delivered, and purified from the influence, oppression, depression, suppression, and regression of satan. I bind ancient strongholds out of my mind. Lord, I choose You, Jesus Christ, to be the Lord over my life, as my personal Savior. I believe You died on the cross for my sins, so I can have a right to eternal life. I believe in the blood atonement of the cross. I believe You are Lord over the entire universe. I believe You can heal and deliver me from all of my troubles. I believe in the power of the Holy Ghost. Your word declares, if I confess with my mouth and believe in my heart that God hath raised Jesus Christ from the dead, I shalt be saved, according to Romans 10:9,

in the Name of Jesus Christ,

Amen!

FOR MORE INFORMATION
VISIT OUR WEBSITE
WWW.DRCHARISSEELEWIS.COM

www.ingramcontent.com/pod-product-compliance
Lightning Source LLC
Chambersburg PA
CBHW021242090426
42740CB00006B/657